# READING STREET
# Sleuth
## COMMON CORE

## PEARSON

**Glenview, Illinois**
**Boston, Massachusetts**
**Chandler, Arizona**
**Upper Saddle River, New Jersey**

Acknowledgments appear on page 78, which constitutes an extension of this copyright page.

ISBN-13: 978-0-328-73056-8
ISBN-10: 0-328-73056-4
4 5 6 7 8 9 10 V003 16 15 14 13 12

# Contents

**From:** The Super Sleuths

**Subject:** Mysteries

Dear Sleuthhound,

A sleuth is a mystery solver. Mysteries are everywhere. There are everyday mysteries that happen in ordinary places. There are mysteries that take place far away in a land that you have never visited. This book is full of mysteries! We need a sleuthhound like you to look for clues. As a sleuth, it's important for you to ask interesting questions. Put all the clues and evidence together. Use the evidence to prove your answers! These Super Sleuth Steps will help you find answers to some great mysteries!

We're counting on you!

# SUPER SLEUTH STEPS

## Gather Evidence

- Look back at the pictures and reread the text. What do the clues tell you?
- Record the evidence. Write or draw what you find.
- Organize the important ideas. Try to put the clues together.

## Ask Questions

- Great questions can be the key to solving a mystery.
- A sleuth is always curious.
- Keep asking questions. Questions can help you learn something amazing.

## Make Your Case

- Look at all the clues. What conclusion can you make?
- State your position clearly. Be ready to convince others.
- Give good reasons to explain your thinking.

## Prove It!

- Show what you have learned. This is your chance to shine!
- You may be working with others. Be certain that everyone has a chance to share the work and the fun!

# Unit 1
## Living and Learning

Hi, Sleuthhounds!
In this unit, you will be looking for clues about how we live and learn. Here are some sleuth tips to help you. Have a great time!

# Sleuth Tips

## Gather Evidence

Where do sleuths find clues?

- Sleuths look for clues as they read. Sometimes clues are easy to find, but other times they are hidden.
- Sleuths look for clues in the pictures. Not all clues are written in the text.

## Ask Questions

What kinds of questions do sleuths ask?

- Sleuths ask many interesting and important questions to find clues!
- Sleuths ask when, where, why, and how something happened.

## Make Your Case

How do sleuths decide on an answer?

- Sleuths look back and reread. Then they think about what they already know.
- Sleuths put the clues together. Clues help them decide on the best answer.

## Prove It!

What do sleuths do to prove what they know?

- Sleuths think about all they have learned and decide which clues are important to share with others.
- Sleuths plan what they will write, draw, or explain. Sleuths check their work to make sure it is clear.

# Dining in the Dark

Have you ever eaten in the dark? For many people, this is a new experience. That is, unless the electricity goes out during dinner.

In 1999, a blind man, Jorge Spielmann, opened the first dark restaurant in Zurich, Switzerland. The Blind Cow was a popular place to eat and still is. It serves people in complete darkness. Only the bathrooms and lobby are lit. Waiters and waitresses, who are also blind, lead customers to and from their seats in darkness. Diners eat in complete darkness too. People discover a new way to enjoy dinner in the dark.

Before opening the restaurant, Spielmann often encouraged guests at his home to eat blindfolded. At many of his dinner parties, his guests enjoyed their meal even more when they were blindfolded.

They focused on the taste of the food. They listened more carefully to what was going on around them. They were not distracted by sights like artwork on the walls or what their friends were wearing.

Today, many people seem excited about dining in the dark. Dark restaurants allow diners to focus on different senses as they eat. At these dark restaurants, no one is worried about when the electricity will come back on! Instead they are enjoying the taste of their food and the conversation of good friends.

## Sleuth Work

**Gather Evidence** How did Spielmann's dinner parties at home lead to the opening of The Blind Cow? Write down evidence from the article to support this.

**Ask Questions** If you could talk to Jorge Spielmann about his restaurant, what would you ask him? Write down three questions you would ask.

**Make Your Case** Would eating without seeing the food make eating more enjoyable or less enjoyable? Why do you think that way? Write a paragraph that supports your opinion.

# I'll Trade You!

Samuel couldn't wait to show his mom and grandma the new skateboard he had just gotten from Ben. Ben couldn't wait to give his sister the new shawl he had just gotten from Samuel. Ben and Samuel were best friends!

Samuel's grandma had worked for weeks knitting the shawl. Ben had wondered for weeks what to get his sister for her birthday. Then one night Ben saw the shawl Samuel's grandma was knitting. He knew his sister would love it!

Samuel spent every day after school skateboarding with Ben. Samuel wished for his own skateboard. Ben knew how much Samuel would love having a skateboard. Suddenly a trade was born!

Trading one thing for another was a way of life. Samuel's mom and grandma remembered when people used something called money instead. Money paid for things they needed. Samuel and Ben were too young to remember that time.

Sometimes, Samuel's mother opened a secret drawer in her jewelry box. She let him hold the shiny coins and smooth dollar bills she had saved. Then they were put away for safekeeping.

People no longer used money. They traded things instead. Samuel couldn't imagine life any other way. Samuel knew how to draw, so he always traded his drawings to get what he wanted. His family and Ben's family traded often. Samuel didn't understand why anyone might need money. Trading was so much easier!

# Sleuth Work

**Gather Evidence** How can you tell that this story takes place some time in the future? Write details that support this.

**Ask Questions** If you could talk with Samuel and Ben, what questions would you ask them about life without money? Write two questions.

**Make Your Case** Would you like to live in a time when there is no money and you have to trade for the things you want or need? List reasons to support your answer.

# A HUNTING LESSON

"Pay attention!" Mama called to her polar bear cubs. The two were playing around rather than listening to Mama's hunting lesson. "One day you will be on your own," she said. "The only way you will survive is if you know how to hunt."

"Yes, Mama," the cubs said. However, before long, they were rolling around on the ice again. They were being cubs. They weren't thinking about how to survive on their own.

"Follow me!" Mama demanded, as she hopped onto an ice floe. Soon the three were drifting out into the ocean.

Mama continued, "The best place to find seals is along cracks in the ice. Seals like to swim under the water, but they must come up for air. They do this along ice cracks."

"That's a good tip, Mama. Where else can we find seals?" one of the cubs asked.

"You might spot them resting in the sun," said Mama.

"Can't we just eat animals that other bears have killed?" asked the other cub.

"That's fine, if and when you find one," said Mama. "Remember, to survive you must work hard. You must think of your best options. You should always have a backup plan if something doesn't work out."

With that, the cubs started rolling around again. Then they fell—*SPLASH*—into the icy water.

"Thank goodness polar bears are good swimmers," Mama thought to herself. It seemed as though the day's hunting lesson was over for now.

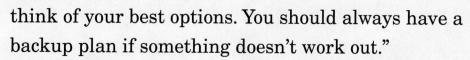

## SLEUTH WORK

**Gather Evidence** Mama described to her cubs where they might look for seals to eat. Name two details that help you visualize where polar bears hunt for seals.

**Ask Questions** If you were one of the polar bear cubs, what questions would you ask your mother about hunting seals? Write two questions.

**Make Your Case** How do you feel about polar bears hunting seals for food? Write your opinion and give two reasons to support your opinion.

# Mackinac Island

Mackinac (pronouced MAH keh NAW) Island is a small island off Michigan's coast. The island is unique. No cars or trucks are allowed! Instead people walk, bicycle, or use a horse-drawn taxi to get around. There are only a few emergency vehicles.

Nearly a million visitors come to the island each summer. They hike in the forests or bike along the coast. Visitors also love the fudge shops. You have to try the fudge! There are at least a half dozen fudge shops on this little island!

It is much easier to visit and live on the island in the summer. Ferries run from Michigan's mainland to the island several times every day. People travel between the mainland and the island to get groceries and other supplies they need.

After summer ends, only several hundred people remain on the island. Getting groceries and other supplies is much more difficult. When the ferries stop running, people can take a small plane to and from the island to carry supplies. It's fast, but not easy to get around.

Usually by February, the lake has frozen and an "ice bridge" forms. You can walk or snowmobile across to the mainland for supplies. How do you think people know if the ice is frozen enough to walk on? Some brave residents check the thickness of the ice and mark a safe path with old Christmas trees.

Mackinac Island is an adventurous place to visit! Make plans to go in the summer when the crossing is safe and easy!

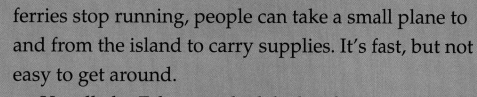

# Sleuth Work

**Gather Evidence** Write three details that support the idea that Mackinac Island is a popular vacation spot.

**Ask Questions** Write three questions that would help you plan a visit to Mackinac Island.

**Make Your Case** Would it be more interesting to visit Mackinac Island in the summer or fall? Support your opinion with three pieces of evidence.

# More Than CASH DISPENSERS

Have you ever visited an ATM? Did you stare in wonder when, like magic, money came out of the machine? Several decades ago banking wasn't so convenient.

People use banks to safely keep and save money. Then, when they need to spend it, they withdraw the money. That's hard to do if your bank isn't nearby. It's even harder to do if your bank is closed. So how do you get cash when you need it?

In the early 1970s, the first ATM, or automated teller machine, was introduced. ATMs are machines. Using a plastic bank card and a PIN, or personal identification number, people can access their bank accounts. They can do this at any time of day or night or even when the bank is closed. They can withdraw money, and they can deposit money and checks. What's even more helpful is that ATMs can be found everywhere!

Banks are adding new ATM services every year. For example, people can now deposit checks without using an envelope. That's because ATMs scan, or read, checks. Another improvement is talking ATMs. These machines have audio, so people who cannot see well or at all can access their bank accounts by listening to instructions.

ATMs keep improving. Some ATMs now have video screens. A banker uses the video screen to talk with the person using the ATM. Other banks are even testing ways mobile phones can be used at ATMs. Just imagine what ATMs will be able to do next!

## SLEUTH WORK

**Gather Evidence** How are modern ATMs different from ATMs from the early 1970s? Give at least one piece of evidence from the text.

**Ask Questions** What ATM service would you like to learn more about? Write a question to guide your research.

**Make Your Case** Will there be a need for bank buildings when you are an adult? Explain your prediction using evidence from the text.

# Unit 2
## Smart Solutions

Hello, Sleuthhounds!
In this unit, you will be looking for clues to learn about smart solutions. Here are some sleuth tips to help you. Ready, set, go!

# Sleuth Tips

## Gather Evidence

Why do sleuths reread?

- Sleuths reread because they know that they may miss something the first time.
- Sleuths focus on finding clues when they reread.

## Ask Questions

What makes a great question?

- Sleuths know that a great question should be focused on the topic.
- Sleuths choose their words carefully to make certain their questions are clear.

## Make Your Case

How do sleuths make a clear case?

- Sleuths make a clear case by using the clues they found in the text.
- Sleuths clearly state what they believe is the answer at the beginning. They state it again at the end.

## Prove It!

What do sleuths do when they work with other sleuths?

- Sleuths share their clues and ideas with other sleuths.
- Sleuths share the work so everyone has an important job to do. Every sleuth is important!

# The Nose Knows

Our noses are a treat for our senses. They inhale the delicious smells of baking cookies and sizzling bacon. They also alert us to danger, such as toast burning in a toaster.

Animals also use their noses to smell. However, some animals use their noses for much more. Have you ever thought about these animals and their odd-shaped noses?

Elephants have a very familiar odd-shaped nose. An elephant's nose, or trunk, is used for touching, tasting, breathing, and drinking. An elephant uses its nose to keep cool in the hot sun. The elephant also uses its nose to get food that cannot be reached without its long trunk.

Elephant Nose Fish

The elephant nose fish is much smaller than a huge elephant. However, its "nose" stands out just the same. Elephant nose fish can be found in muddy waters in Africa. This fish uses its long "nose" to find food in the mud.

The hammerhead shark uses its nose to find prey too. The shark's favorite meal is stingrays. A hammerhead uses its snout to dig stingrays out of their hiding places in the sand.

Then there's the star-nosed mole. This animal has one bizarre nose! Its nose is covered with 22 tentacles. These tentacles help the mole find its food really quickly. Insects and worms are a mole's favorite meal. With this nose, worms and insects can't hide! This is definitely a nose that knows.

Hammerhead Shark

Star-nosed Mole

## Sleuth Work

**Gather Evidence** What details help you understand that noses are used for more than smelling? List three details.

**Ask Questions** What questions would you want to research to discover more about one of these animals? Write three questions.

**Make Your Case** Which of these animals has the most interesting nose? Support your answer by listing details from the article.

# Don't Give Up!

What do Sonia Sotomayor, Walt Disney, Dr. Seuss, and Thomas Edison have in common? They have become famous successful people—but they didn't start out that way!

Sonia Sotomayor has overcome many challenges. She grew up poor and lost her father when she was young. She spoke only Spanish as a child. However, she studied hard in school and became a lawyer. Today she serves on the United States Supreme Court. She is only the third woman to do so.

Sonia Sotomayor

Walt Disney was fired from his newspaper job and told he had a poor imagination. Today, Disney's ideas inspire theme parks and a movie company.

Theodor Geisel, also known as Dr. Seuss, wrote his first book called *And to Think That I Saw It on Mulberry Street.* After 27 different book companies turned it down, one company printed it. He went on to write over 40 children's books.

These people might have just given up, but they *didn't*. They kept trying and became successful.

Thomas Edison didn't give up, either. He invented many things, including

Walt Disney

improvements to the light bulb. It took him hundreds of tries before he found the materials that worked best for this invention. He never thought of himself as a failure. He said, "I have not failed. I've just found 10,000 ways that won't work."

Every time Edison tried something that didn't work, he got one step closer to finding a way that *would* work.

So the next time you're trying to learn something new or solve a problem, don't stop trying. You may be just one step away from success!

Dr. Seuss

Thomas Edison

# Sleuth Work

**Ask Questions** If you could talk to one of the famous people mentioned in this article, whom would you talk to and what would you ask? Make a list of the questions you would like to ask.

**Gather Evidence** How does the author feel about failure? Write sentences from the article that support your answer.

**Make Your Case** Is determination or skill a more important factor in being successful? Make a list of reasons to support your opinions.

# Getting ORGANIZED

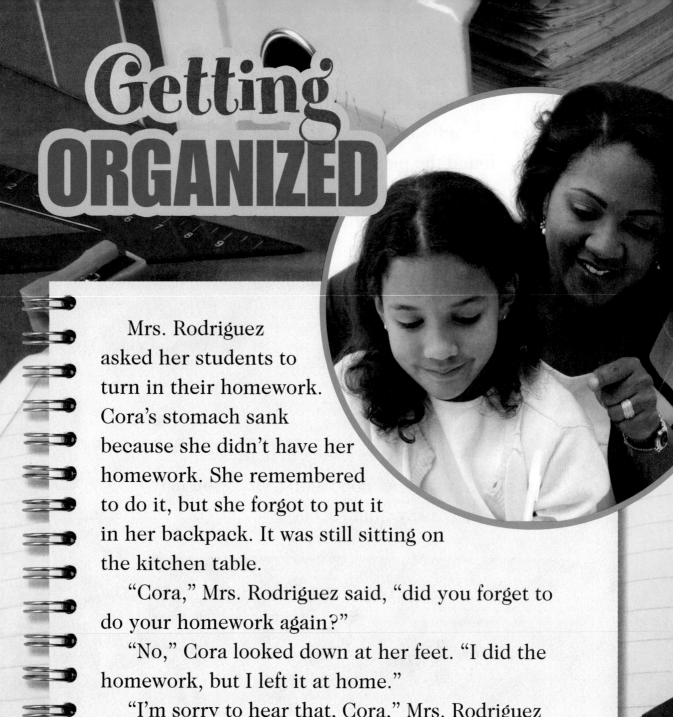

Mrs. Rodriguez asked her students to turn in their homework. Cora's stomach sank because she didn't have her homework. She remembered to do it, but she forgot to put it in her backpack. It was still sitting on the kitchen table.

"Cora," Mrs. Rodriguez said, "did you forget to do your homework again?"

"No," Cora looked down at her feet. "I did the homework, but I left it at home."

"I'm sorry to hear that, Cora," Mrs. Rodriguez said. "Bring it in tomorrow, but you will lose five points."

That night the phone rang. "Hello, Mrs. Rodriguez," Cora heard her mother answer. *This cannot be good,* Cora thought.

"Of course, I will talk to Cora."

"Cora," Mama said, "Mrs. Rodriguez says your missing and late assignments are going to affect your grade. That's a problem."

"I'm sorry," Cora said. "I'm always in such a rush in the morning. It's hard to remember everything."

"Cora, rather than being sorry," Mama said, "I want you to solve this problem. You're too smart to let a lack of organization get in the way of good grades."

"What can I do, Mama?" Cora asked.

"Let's think of some ways you can be more organized," Mama said.

Cora came up with three solutions to her problem:
1. Write down my assignments.
2. Get ready for school the night before.
3. Have Mama double-check my homework.

Three weeks later, Cora brought home her report card. Mama gave her a hug. Cora's solutions had worked!

# Sleuth Work

**Gather Evidence** Cora has been disorganized for a while. Write two details from the story that let you know about this problem.

**Ask Questions** What questions might the teacher have asked Cora to help understand why Cora's homework wasn't turned in on time? Write two questions.

**Make Your Case** Do you think Cora's solutions would work for everyone? Write your opinion and support it with at least two reasons.

# THE Election

It was time for the school elections. Each class voted on who would represent it in the school congress. A committee was formed of third, fourth, and fifth graders. Its job was to choose the best voting process. Everyone had ideas about how the voting should be done.

Anton, a fifth grader, thought everyone should fill out a ballot. The voting station would be in the school cafeteria. At lunch, each student would write a candidate's name on a piece of paper and put it into a box. Then the votes would be counted.

Nisha, a fourth grader, thought that each class should vote for a representative. Then each grade would vote for those winners to select a representative for each grade.

Scotty, a third grader, thought that each grade should have an assembly to choose its representative. Someone would call out a candidate's name. Then students would raise their hands if they wanted that person to represent them. The person who got the most hands raised would be the winner.

The students went round and round about what they should do. Finally, they asked a teacher for her thoughts. "We're having a hard time agreeing on the voting process for the election," they said to the teacher.

"Why not vote on it?" asked Mrs. Hanson.

## Sleuth Work

**Gather Evidence** The election committee had several ideas for the voting process. How were they all alike? Write details that support this.

**Ask Questions** When the committee asked the teacher for help, what questions might she have asked the committee to help it reach a decision? Write two of those questions.

**Make Your Case** Which method of voting do you think is the best? Why? Write your opinion and give a reason to support it.

# I Spy

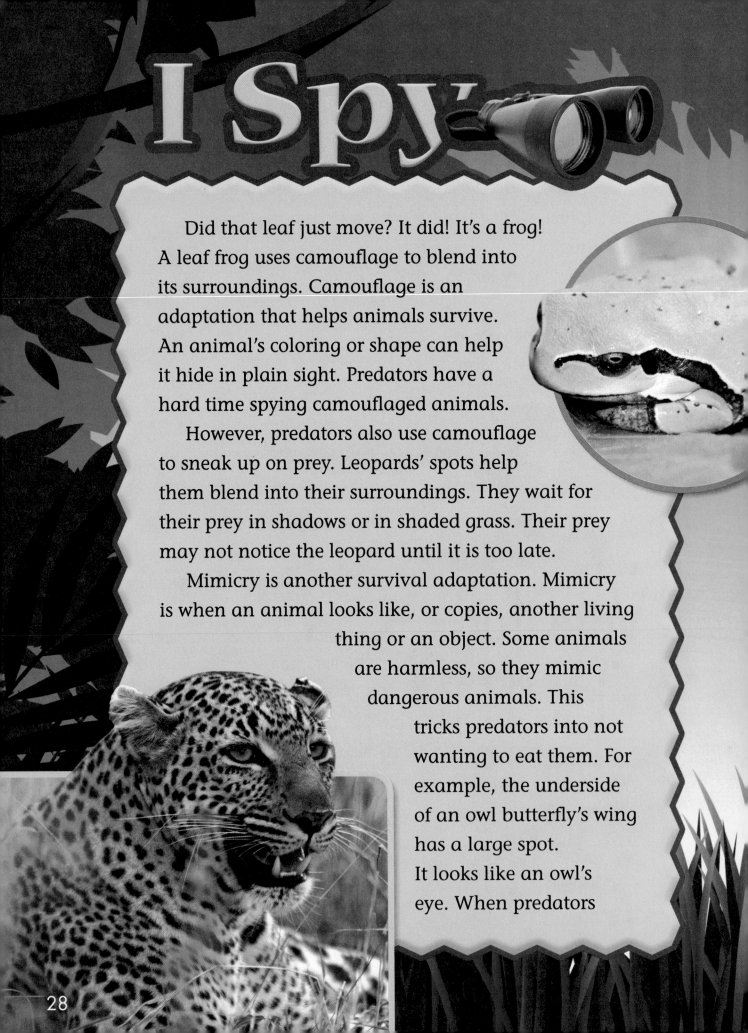

Did that leaf just move? It did! It's a frog! A leaf frog uses camouflage to blend into its surroundings. Camouflage is an adaptation that helps animals survive. An animal's coloring or shape can help it hide in plain sight. Predators have a hard time spying camouflaged animals.

However, predators also use camouflage to sneak up on prey. Leopards' spots help them blend into their surroundings. They wait for their prey in shadows or in shaded grass. Their prey may not notice the leopard until it is too late.

Mimicry is another survival adaptation. Mimicry is when an animal looks like, or copies, another living thing or an object. Some animals are harmless, so they mimic dangerous animals. This tricks predators into not wanting to eat them. For example, the underside of an owl butterfly's wing has a large spot. It looks like an owl's eye. When predators see the butterfly, they are scared off. They are fooled into thinking the butterfly is an owl, a creature that might attack them instead. By looking like this animal, owl butterflies have a better chance of surviving.

Predators also use mimicry to attract prey. An alligator snapping turtle has a tongue that looks like a worm. Fish like to eat worms, and snapping turtles like to eat fish! These turtles use their tongues to catch fish. Chomp!

Camouflage and mimicry are adaptations that help animals survive. Next time you are outside see what animals you can spy.

## Sleuth Work

**Gather Evidence** How are camouflage and mimicry alike and different? Make a Venn diagram.

**Ask Questions** Write an interesting question about one of the animals that uses mimicry or camouflage. Where could you find the answer to your question?

**Make Your Case** Which do you think is more useful, camouflage or mimicry? Using details from the text, explain your reasoning.

# Unit 3
## People and Nature

Hello, Sleuthhounds!

In this unit, you will be looking for clues about people and nature. Here are some sleuth tips to help you. Good luck!

# Sleuth Tips

## Gather Evidence

How do sleuths get clues from pictures?

- Sleuths use pictures to help them understand. Pictures can help explain harder words or ideas.
- Sleuths look at pictures to learn things that may not be included in the text.

## Ask Questions

Why are sleuths so curious?

- Sleuths are always wondering. They try to find hidden clues by asking questions.
- Sleuths know that being curious and asking questions can lead to answers and adventures!

## Make Your Case

Why don't all sleuths agree on the answers?

- Sleuths may find different clues, or they may put the same clues together in different ways.
- Sleuths know that everyone has different experiences. Our unique experiences cause each of us to think differently.

## Prove It!

How can sleuths be creative when showing what they have learned?

- Sleuths are unique! They use new and different ways to show details clearly.
- Sleuths are creative! They think of different ways to share what they know.

# BOG SWEET BOG

It's fall harvest time down on the cranberry bog. The cranberries are dark red. It's time to harvest!

There are two ways to harvest cranberries. Wet harvesting is when part of the bog is purposely flooded. A machine called a water reel beats the vines. It helps cranberries pull away from the vines and float to the surface of the water. The floating cranberries are collected. Then the fruit is loaded onto trucks.

Next, cranberries have to be washed to remove leaves and dirt. The good berries are pulled out from the bad berries. Good berries bounce along a separator. Bad berries do not bounce and get thrown out.

Finally, the wet harvested cranberries reach your supermarket. You'll find these berries as canned cranberries, cranberry sauce, and cranberry juice.

Dry harvesting is another way to harvest cranberries. The bogs are not flooded. Instead a machine picks cranberries off the vines. This machine looks like a giant lawnmower! As the machine picks cranberries, it lifts the fruit into a container.

The dry harvested cranberries are also washed. Good berries are separated from bad berries. Soft brushes polish the fruit. Dry harvested cranberries are sold at your supermarket as fresh cranberries. They are often packaged in bags and found in the produce section of the supermarket.

No matter how cranberries are harvested, they are tasty to drink or eat as part of a Thanksgiving feast. They can also be found in yummy holiday goodies!

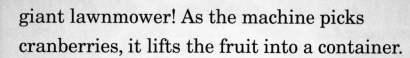

# SLEUTH WORK

**Gather Evidence** What clues can you find about the sequence of events when cranberries are harvested? Write down a list of sequence words that helped you to understand the harvesting procedure.

**Ask Questions** What would you ask a farmer about harvesting cranberries? Write down at least one opinion question and one factual question.

**Make Your Case** What kind of harvesting, wet or dry, do you think is more difficult? Include at least two facts that support your opinion.

# ATHENA and ARACHNE

There once lived a lovely girl named Arachne (uh-RAK-nee). She was known far and wide for her weaving skills. Arachne knew she was good at weaving. She bragged about it, saying she was the best in the world. She said she was even better than Athena (a-THEE-na), the goddess of wisdom and crafts.

Athena heard about Arachne's bragging. Athena disguised herself as an old woman and visited Arachne. The old woman warned the girl not to be too proud. She reminded Arachne that humans must never say they are better than the gods. She gave Arachne a chance to apologize. Arachne did not. In fact, Arachne challenged Athena to a contest.

In an instant, Athena turned herself back into a goddess. The contest began. Athena began weaving a picture of powerful gods and the foolish humans who challenged them.

It was her way of giving Arachne one last warning. Arachne did not notice. She was busy weaving a picture of gods and goddesses looking silly and doing foolish things.

Athena became terribly angry. She sprinkled a magic potion on the young girl. Arachne instantly became a very small, ugly insect. Her hair fell out. Her fingers became legs that were attached to her sides. Arachne was turned into a spider.

From that day on, Arachne and all of her family were doomed to weave webs and live in them forever. Humans would think spiders were ugly and try to destroy their weaving. In this way, no one would forget the lesson learned from Arachne's misfortune.

## Sleuth Work

**Gather Evidence** What evidence do you find in the text that lets you know this is a myth?

**Ask Questions** Write two interesting questions you have about spiders. Where could you find the answers to your questions?

**Make Your Case** At what point does taking pride in your work become a problem? Give evidence from the text and your own experiences to explain your thinking.

# Pictures in the Night Sky

Pictures are all around you. You draw pictures and pictures may decorate the walls of your home. You can also see pictures in the night sky. These pictures are made up of stars. They are called constellations. They have names like the Big Dipper, the Little Dipper, Leo the Lion, and Pisces the Fish.

Constellations are actually random groupings of stars that look like things or creatures to people. Both farmers and other people have observed the stars for thousands of years. Over time they have given the groupings of stars names that describe what they look like. Naming the groups of stars wasn't just a fun thing to do, though.

Because it's hard to tell the stars apart, people came up with names for these constellations. It's a way to know which star is which.

Why does it help to tell the stars apart? Long ago, there were no calendars to tell farmers what the current month was.

Instead, farmers used stars to know when it was time to plant and harvest crops. As the Earth revolves around the sun, we who live on the Earth see the stars in different places in the night sky. The stars in the night sky appear to change locations throughout the year. Farmers came up with the idea of looking at the constellations as a way to tell the stars apart, and thus what time of year it was. So the next time you look up at the stars, look to see what pictures you can find in the sky.

# Sleuth Work

**Gather Evidence** How did constellations come about? Write down evidence from the article to support this.

**Ask Questions** Write down two questions you would ask about constellations.

**Make Your Case** Since farmers have calendars now to decide when to plant and harvest crops, is there still a reason to be interested in constellations? Write a paragraph that supports your opinion.

# A Whale of a Rescue

Imagine walking along the beach and stopping now and then to pick up an interesting shell. You see something at the water's edge. You realize it's a whale—a whale stranded on the beach.

Some animals, such as seals, often come out of the water onto the shore. But for whales, dolphins, and porpoises, this behavior usually means that something is wrong. Sometimes the animal is sick, but sometimes it has just lost its way. Swimming in stormy seas can exhaust some animals. Their exhaustion will make them disoriented. Others get stuck in shallow waters when the tide is outgoing.

One time, in February 2011, not just one whale, but 82 were stranded! For reasons unknown, 82 pilot whales became stranded on a beach in New Zealand.

The Department of Conservation of New Zealand, along with over 100 volunteers, came to the rescue. They worked all weekend long to get the animals back into the water. All but 17 whales made it.

Then, just days later, 65 whales were stranded again! This time, the volunteers didn't try to move the whales back into the water. "New evidence suggests that moving stranded whales causes them a lot of stress and pain," Department of Conservation ranger Simon Walls told a local newspaper. Instead, the volunteers cared for the whales on shore while waiting for the high tides to return.

All 65 of the newly-stranded whales were successfully returned to the water. The plan had worked!

# Sleuth Work

**Gather Evidence** What evidence can you find in the text to explain why whales might become stranded on the beach?

**Ask Questions** Write three questions about the stranded pilot whales and the people who tried to help them.

**Make Your Case** Do you think it is wise for people to change the outcome of natural events or should people let events happen without interfering? Provide two convincing reasons for your opinion.

# BACKYARD SAFARI

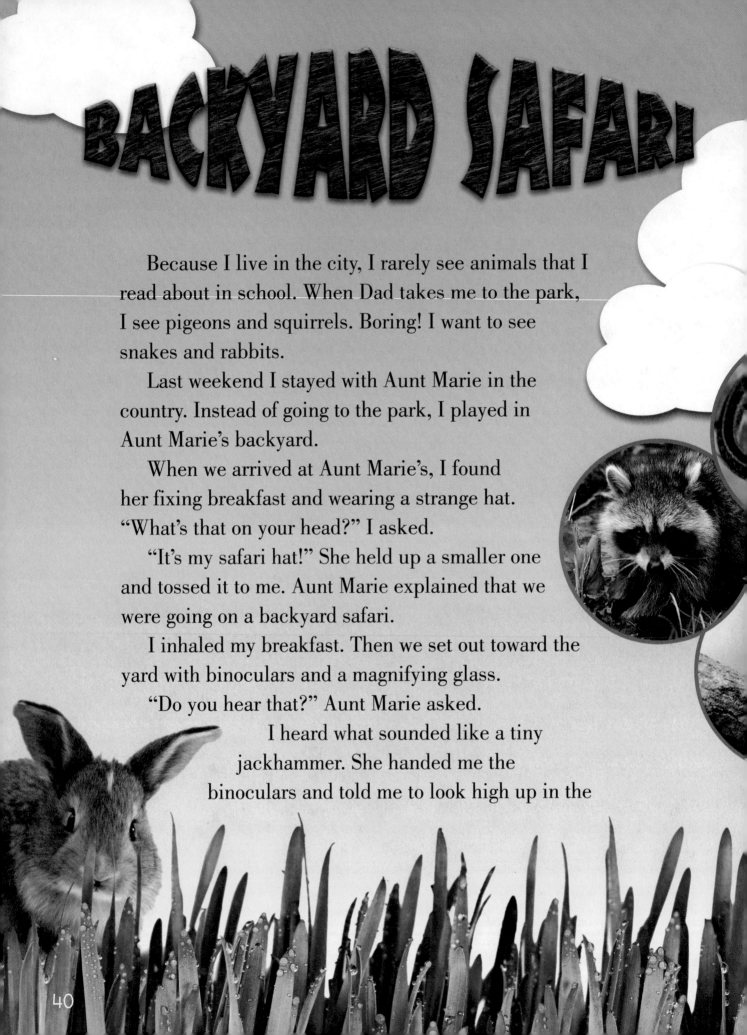

Because I live in the city, I rarely see animals that I read about in school. When Dad takes me to the park, I see pigeons and squirrels. Boring! I want to see snakes and rabbits.

Last weekend I stayed with Aunt Marie in the country. Instead of going to the park, I played in Aunt Marie's backyard.

When we arrived at Aunt Marie's, I found her fixing breakfast and wearing a strange hat. "What's that on your head?" I asked.

"It's my safari hat!" She held up a smaller one and tossed it to me. Aunt Marie explained that we were going on a backyard safari.

I inhaled my breakfast. Then we set out toward the yard with binoculars and a magnifying glass.

"Do you hear that?" Aunt Marie asked.

I heard what sounded like a tiny jackhammer. She handed me the binoculars and told me to look high up in the tree. I soon found the source of the noise. It was a woodpecker with a red head.

Aunt Marie said that rabbits love to rest under her rose bushes. We lay in the grass and waited. As we waited, she told me all about the critters that call her backyard home—opossum, raccoons, chipmunks, and snakes. Some like to come out early in the morning, others at night.

Then something caught my eye. It was a ball of fur with a nose that was wiggling. "A rabbit," I whispered, even though I wanted to yell. Who knew I could see so much wildlife on a backyard safari!

# SLEUTH WORK

**Gather Evidence** Write two clues that show the narrator was excited about the backyard safari.

**Ask Questions** Write two questions that you would ask an expert about animals that live near humans.

**Make Your Case** In your town or community, where is the best place to go on a safari? List evidence to support your answer.

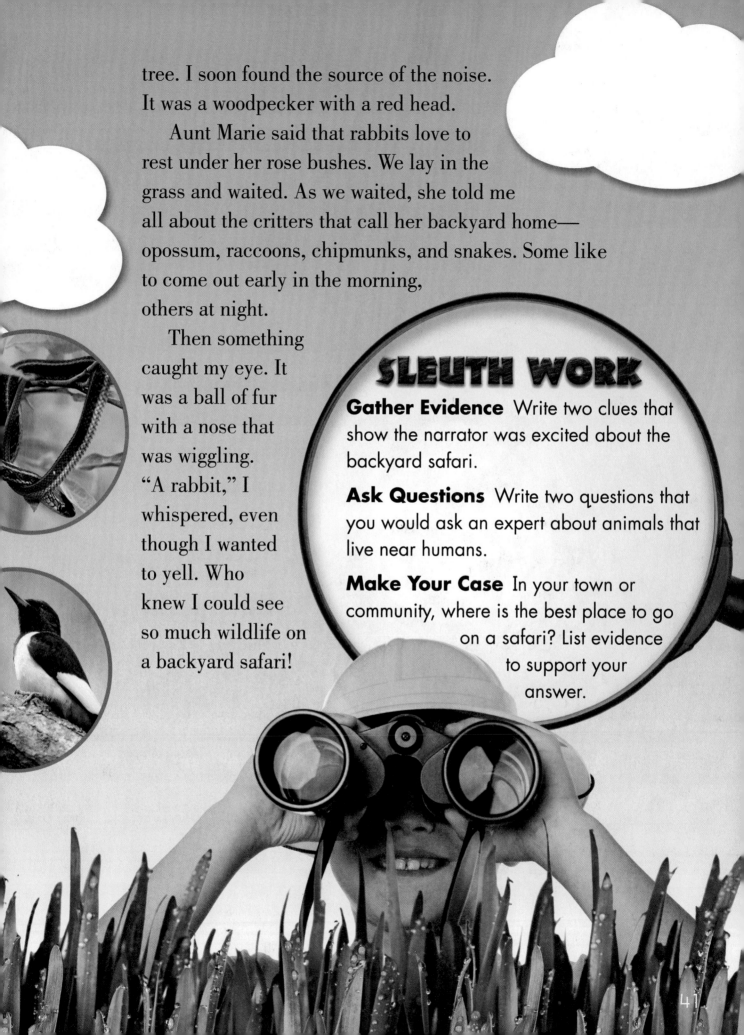

# Unit 4
## One of a Kind

Hi, Sleuthhounds!
In this unit, you will be looking for clues about how something is one of a kind. Here are some sleuth tips to help you. Be unique!

# Sleuth Tips

## Gather Evidence

How do sleuths remember clues?

- Sleuths don't expect to remember everything they read and see. They write down important details.
- Sleuths might write a list or draw a picture to help them remember clues.

## Ask Questions

Why do sleuths ask questions?

- Sleuths ask questions to gather facts and details about a topic.
- Sleuths ask questions to make everyone think harder or differently.

## Make Your Case

How do sleuths disagree with other sleuths?

- Sleuths know that everyone is unique and that not everyone will agree. They want to hear lots of ideas.
- Sleuths discuss clues with others to find areas of agreement.

## Prove It!

What do sleuths think about before they share?

- Sleuths review what they have learned before they present it.
- Sleuths consider what is most important to include and what can be left out.

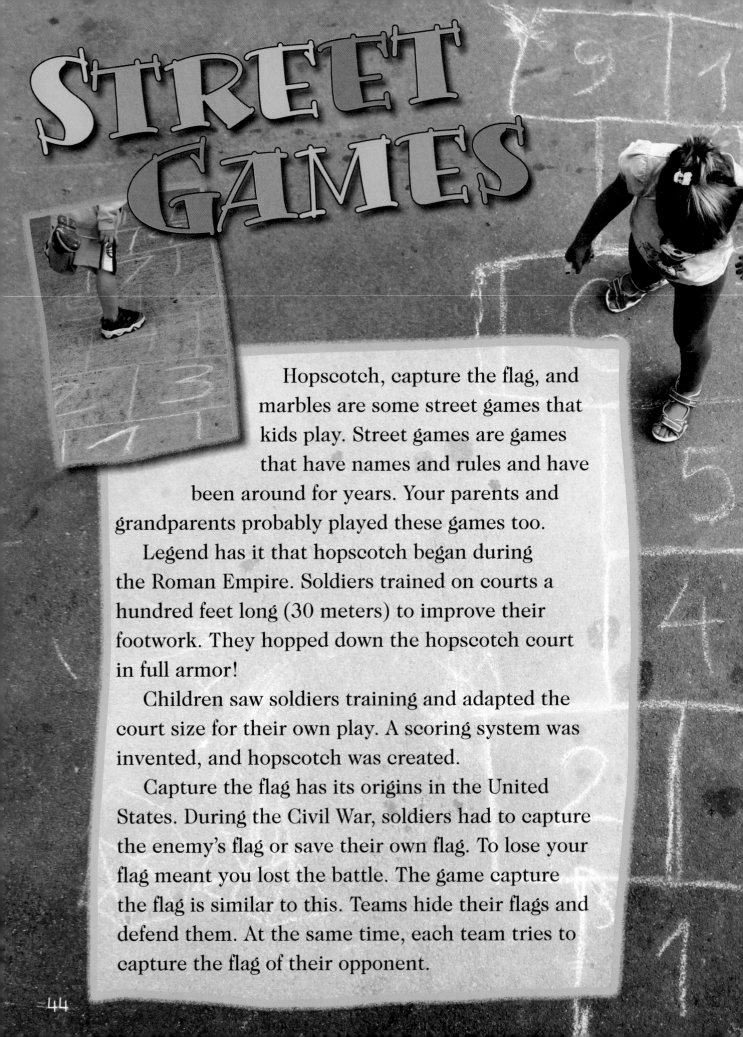

# STREET GAMES

Hopscotch, capture the flag, and marbles are some street games that kids play. Street games are games that have names and rules and have been around for years. Your parents and grandparents probably played these games too.

Legend has it that hopscotch began during the Roman Empire. Soldiers trained on courts a hundred feet long (30 meters) to improve their footwork. They hopped down the hopscotch court in full armor!

Children saw soldiers training and adapted the court size for their own play. A scoring system was invented, and hopscotch was created.

Capture the flag has its origins in the United States. During the Civil War, soldiers had to capture the enemy's flag or save their own flag. To lose your flag meant you lost the battle. The game capture the flag is similar to this. Teams hide their flags and defend them. At the same time, each team tries to capture the flag of their opponent.

The game of marbles also dates back to the time of the Roman Empire. Marbles during this time were made of stone, baked clay, and marble itself. Early on, a player rolled a large marble across the ground to begin the game. Then players would try to hit the large marble with their smaller marbles. The player closest to the large marble was the winner. Today, kids play many different marble games that are similar.

Street games continue to entertain kids of all ages. Most likely your kids will play these games someday too.

# SLEUTH WORK

**Gather Evidence** Many street games have been around for a long time. Make a list of evidence that supports this statement.

**Ask Questions** What questions might you ask your parents or grandparents about the street games they played as kids? Write down three questions.

**Make Your Case** Will these games still be played by future generations of kids? State reasons for your opinion.

# The Wettest Place on Earth

Olivia and her family were on vacation in Hawaii. They were staying on the island of Kauai (kuh WY ee). Today they were taking a helicopter tour of the island. They would be flying over its jagged mountains and steep cliffs.

Olivia couldn't wait to see Mt. Waialeale (wy ALL ay ALL ay). That means "rippling waters" in Hawaiian. Waialeale is one of the wettest places on Earth because of the amount of rain it gets. It gets more than 450 inches (1,143 centimeters) a year! There is a small lake at the top of an extinct volcano.

The plane flew toward the center of the island. Olivia looked down at the lush green forests that her family loved so much. Soon the helicopter reached Mt. Waialeale. The pilot pointed out where the official rain gauge is set up to measure the rainfall. He said that scientists have to fly in to check the gauge because it's nearly impossible to hike up the volcano. The sides of the old volcano are very steep and slippery because they're so wet.

Humans have walked up the volcano despite the hazards, though. The pilot even pointed out the remains of a small altar that had been built by ancient Hawaiians. Olivia and her family also saw a small wooden statue that had been left there by a more recent visitor.

From her perch high in the sky, Olivia looked down at one of the wettest places on Earth. She thought it might also be one of the most beautiful places on Earth.

# Sleuth Work

**Gather Evidence** Which parts of this story might be fact? Which parts are opinion? Make a T-chart that lists the facts and opinions of this story.

**Ask Questions** If you could talk to someone who managed to make the difficult hike up to Mt. Waialeale, what would you ask that person? Write down three questions you would ask.

**Make Your Case** What is the best way to explore a place you're visiting for the first time? Write reasons that support your answer.

# Rocks and More Rocks

"Patrick, your room looks like a rock quarry," Mom said as she stepped over a pile of rocks.

"I know," Patrick said. "It's awesome!"

"It's a neat collection, Patrick, but it's taking over your room. Maybe it's time to start weeding some out."

"I wouldn't know which ones to get rid of," Patrick complained.

That afternoon Patrick and his mom were gardening when their neighbor Mrs. Simpson stopped by. Mrs. Simpson worked at the nature center.

"What are you planting today?" she asked.

Patrick spoke up. "Mom's planting peppers and I'm digging for rocks."

"Patrick's rock collection keeps growing," Mom added. "Why don't you show Mrs. Simpson your collection, Patrick?"

Patrick led Mrs. Simpson to his room. Mrs. Simpson's eyes grew big when she saw all the rocks.

"Wow, Patrick, this is quite a collection!" she said. "Do you know what kind of rocks you have?"

"No, they're just rocks," Patrick said.

"Well, it may be interesting to know which minerals are in those rocks. Minerals are the building blocks of rocks."

"Mom wants me to get rid of some of my rocks," Patrick said.

"Patrick, come to the nature center. You can look through field guides to see what you have. Once you have learned more about the rocks, you may find some to get rid of. A good rock collector learns to be particular about his rocks."

"Wow," said Patrick, "I didn't realize there was so much to collecting rocks. I'll see you at the nature center!"

# Sleuth Works

**Gather Evidence** Did Patrick's mom support his desire to collect rocks? Write down evidence from the article.

**Ask Questions** Write two questions you might ask Mrs. Simpson about her job at the nature center.

**Make Your Case** Do you think rocks or coins would make a more interesting collection? Write a paragraph that supports your opinion. Use evidence from the story.

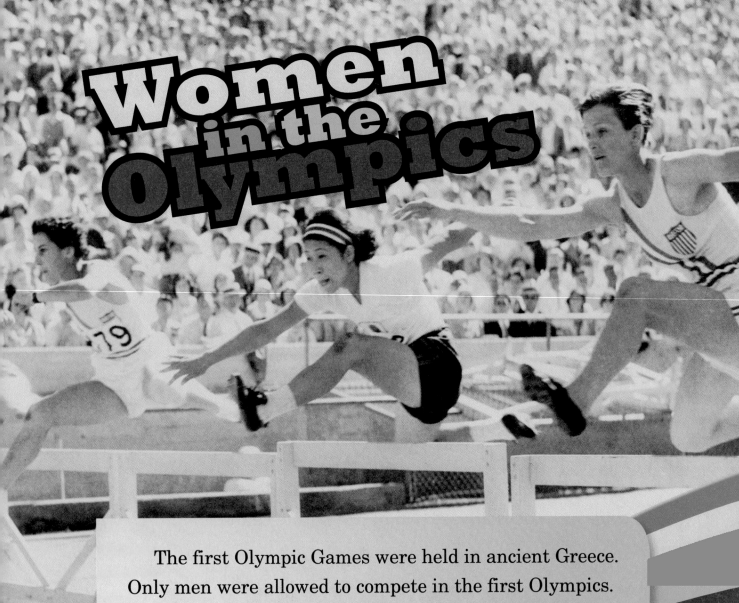

# Women in the Olympics

The first Olympic Games were held in ancient Greece. Only men were allowed to compete in the first Olympics. Women weren't even allowed to watch men wrestle, box, or run in a foot race!

That changed in the 1900 Olympic Games in Paris, France. Women were allowed to compete. Eleven women played lawn tennis and golf. England's Charlotte Cooper won the first tennis match that year.

In 1912, women entered swimming events in the Olympics. However, American women could only compete in events in which they wore long skirts to cover their legs. Because of this rule, there were no American women swimmers in the 1912 Olympic Games.

In 1928, women began to compete in Olympic track and field events. One event, the 800-meter race, took its toll on the women. Many women collapsed at the end of the race. Because of this, this race was canceled for women until 1960.

In 1952, women made a real impact in the Olympics. A Soviet gymnast won two gold medals and five silver medals. This was the best performance by any athlete, male or female, that year! It was also the first time the gymnast's country had anyone compete at the Olympics.

Today women break barriers and records at the Olympics Games. Women can compete in nearly every Olympic sport.

# Sleuth Work

**Gather Evidence** Early in Olympic history, women from around the world did not seem to have equal standing with men from around the world. What evidence in the text supports this idea? Write your answer.

**Ask Questions** Write three interesting questions about the history of the Olympics. Where could you find an answer to one of the questions?

**Make Your Case** Are there any sports that should be open only to males or females? Why or why not? Support your opinion with three strong reasons.

# Communicating Without Words

How would you communicate if you couldn't speak or use sign language? Animals can't speak, so they use visuals, sounds, and touch to communicate. You may be wondering what an animal possibly has to say—a lot actually!

Peacocks and fireflies use visuals to attract mates. Male peacocks are known for their beautiful, colorful feathers. They fan out their feathers. Then they parade in front of females. Male fireflies use light to attract females. A male signals with light to a female. She responds by flashing her own light. Light and color are visuals that allow these animals to communicate.

Under the sea and in the sky, whales and birds communicate using sound. Whales, such as the humpback whale, use sounds called phonations. Some phonations are too low or too high for humans to hear. Whales make these sounds to keep in contact with other whales. The sounds can reach whales that may be as far away as 50 miles (80 kilometers).

SIGHT

SOUND

The songs and calls that birds make can be beautiful. But did you know this is how birds communicate? Birds sing and call for many reasons. They may sing to attract a mate or call to warn off a predator.

Elephants use sound to communicate, but they also use touch. A mother elephant uses her trunk to gently stroke her calf or to discipline it. Two elephants greet each other with their trunks. They place the tip of the trunk in the other's mouth. It's like an elephant saying, "Hello!"

# Sleuth Work

**Gather Evidence** How do animals communicate without words? Write three details from the article.

**Ask Questions** What animal communication method would you like to learn more about? Write three questions to guide your inquiry.

**Make Your Case** Which method of animal communication from the text is most similar to how people communicate? Support your opinion with two pieces of evidence.

# Unit 5
## Cultures

Hello, Sleuthhounds!

In this unit, you will be looking for clues about cultures. Here are some sleuth tips to help you. Way to go!

# Sleuth Tips

## Gather Evidence

How do sleuths find clues given by authors?

- Sleuths look for sequence clues, how one event caused another, or how one event had many effects.
- Sleuths think hard while they read and put different clues together.

## Ask Questions

Where do sleuths get answers to their questions?

- Sleuths find answers to their questions in pictures, in the text, and by talking to other sleuths.
- Sleuths use books or computers to find answers. A good sleuth never gives up!

## Make Your Case

How do sleuths use clues when they make a case?

- Sleuths explain how the clues led them to their conclusions.
- Sleuths know that it's important to explain how pictures and text reveal answers.

## Prove It!

Why do sleuths think about who will read what they write?

- Sleuths know that readers are different and that one type of writing will not always work.
- Sleuths always try to be interesting and clear.

# Celebrating Children and Tradition

Each year on May 5 Japan celebrates children. The holiday is called Children's Day. My friend Akiko is from Japan. She invited me to come to her home to celebrate with her.

When I got to Akiko's house, everyone was wearing kimonos because it was a special day. I borrowed one to wear. Akiko told me that kimonos have been part of Japanese culture for more than 1,000 years. Some of the kimonos were very colorful.

Akiko's mom told me that different colors and patterns show a person's social status, military rank, age, or gender. A kimono with many layers may mean the person is wealthy.

At Akiko's house, I saw large fish-shaped banners hanging from the doorway. As the wind caught them, they looked like they were flying. Akiko explained they were a type of fish called carp. She said that carp are strong and able to swim against strong river currents to get where they want to go. Carp symbolize parents' wishes for their children to grow up strong too.

Akiko said, "That's what Children's Day is all about. It celebrates the strength and health of children."

Then Akiko led us into the backyard. There we discovered lots of outdoor activities. Akiko said that each year on Children's Day Japan holds the Kids' Olympics. Akiko's family held their own Kids' Olympics. Even dressed in kimonos all of the children ran fast! It was a close finish, but Akiko and I won first place in the relay race!

## Sleuth Work

**Gather Evidence** What evidence can you find to show the importance of wearing kimonos in Japan?

**Ask Questions** Write two interesting questions you have about kimonos.

**Make Your Case** Describe a new holiday you think should be celebrated in your hometown. Explain why it should be celebrated, and describe the special clothing people should wear.

# A Visit to Vietnam

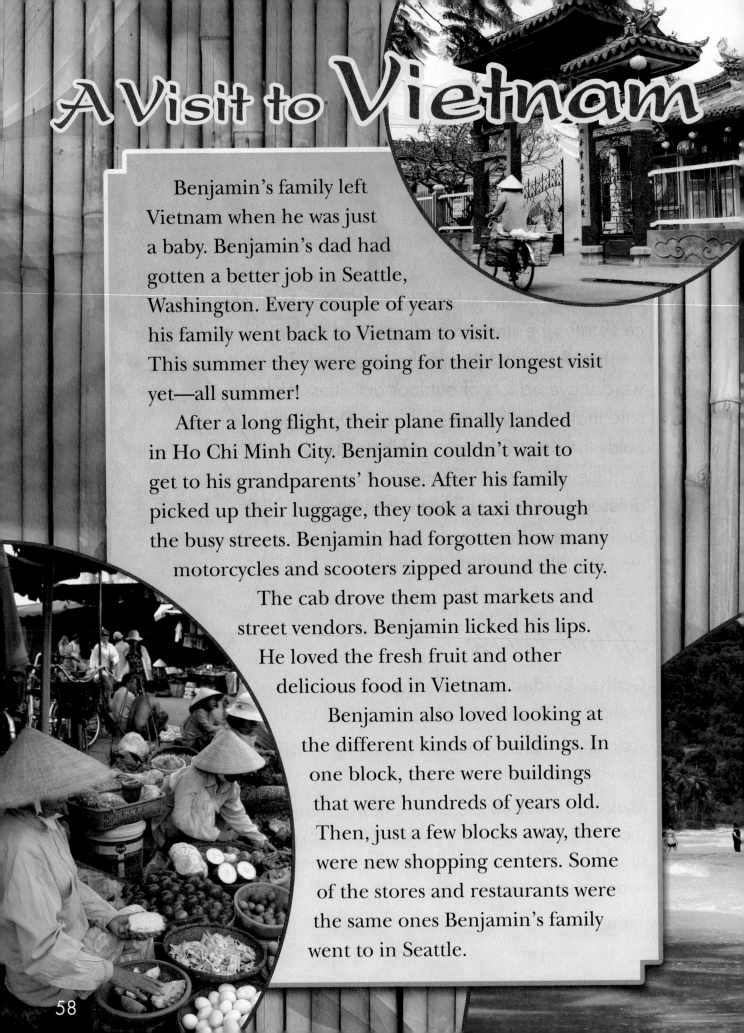

Benjamin's family left Vietnam when he was just a baby. Benjamin's dad had gotten a better job in Seattle, Washington. Every couple of years his family went back to Vietnam to visit. This summer they were going for their longest visit yet—all summer!

After a long flight, their plane finally landed in Ho Chi Minh City. Benjamin couldn't wait to get to his grandparents' house. After his family picked up their luggage, they took a taxi through the busy streets. Benjamin had forgotten how many motorcycles and scooters zipped around the city.

The cab drove them past markets and street vendors. Benjamin licked his lips. He loved the fresh fruit and other delicious food in Vietnam.

Benjamin also loved looking at the different kinds of buildings. In one block, there were buildings that were hundreds of years old. Then, just a few blocks away, there were new shopping centers. Some of the stores and restaurants were the same ones Benjamin's family went to in Seattle.

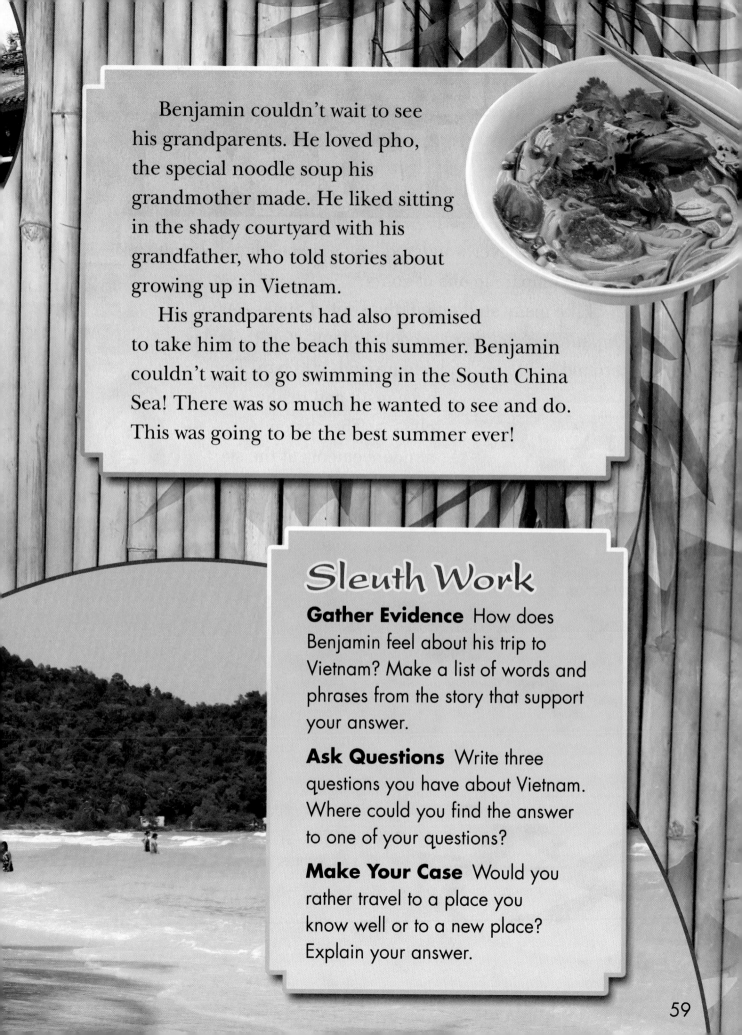

Benjamin couldn't wait to see his grandparents. He loved pho, the special noodle soup his grandmother made. He liked sitting in the shady courtyard with his grandfather, who told stories about growing up in Vietnam.

His grandparents had also promised to take him to the beach this summer. Benjamin couldn't wait to go swimming in the South China Sea! There was so much he wanted to see and do. This was going to be the best summer ever!

## Sleuth Work

**Gather Evidence** How does Benjamin feel about his trip to Vietnam? Make a list of words and phrases from the story that support your answer.

**Ask Questions** Write three questions you have about Vietnam. Where could you find the answer to one of your questions?

**Make Your Case** Would you rather travel to a place you know well or to a new place? Explain your answer.

# A Day at School in Japan

Have you ever wondered how a school day in Japan might compare to one of yours?

Like many students in the United States, many Japanese elementary school students start their day around 8:30 a.m. and end around 3:00 p.m. They have math and reading classes. They listen to announcements at the start of the day. The teacher takes attendance. During the week, students might gather for an assembly where the principal or someone else talks to them.

There are a number of differences too. For example, in the United States, students learn handwriting. In Japan, students learn *shodo*, or calligraphy. This involves dipping a brush into ink and writing symbols. The symbols stand for words. Students in Japan also have a class where they learn how to cook and sew.

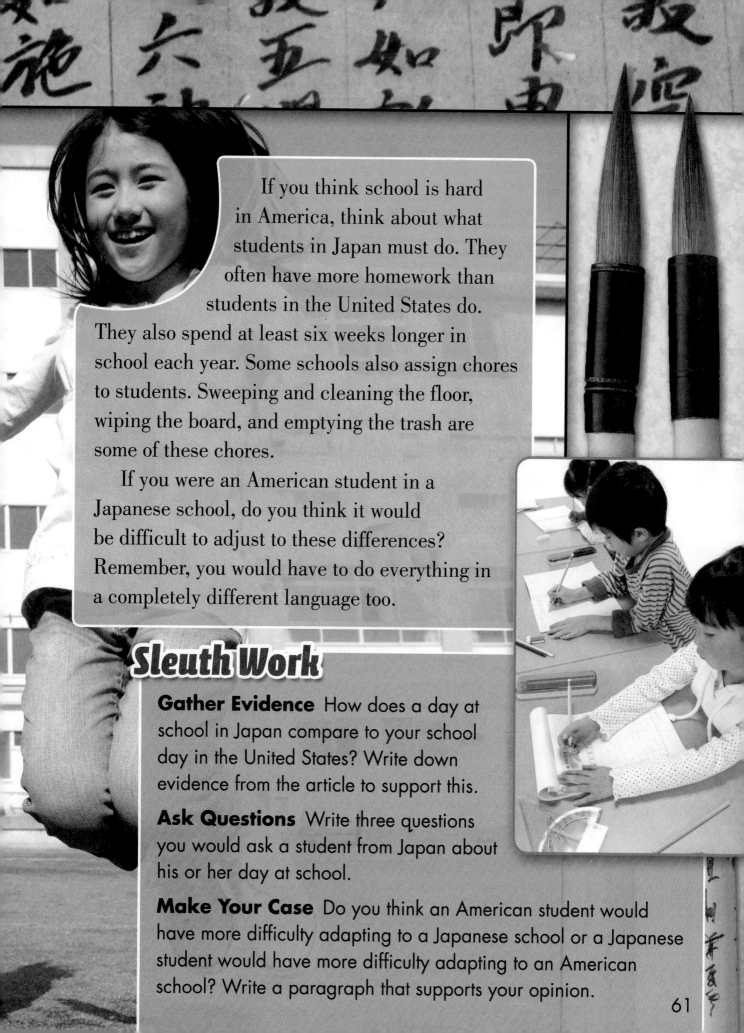

If you think school is hard in America, think about what students in Japan must do. They often have more homework than students in the United States do. They also spend at least six weeks longer in school each year. Some schools also assign chores to students. Sweeping and cleaning the floor, wiping the board, and emptying the trash are some of these chores.

If you were an American student in a Japanese school, do you think it would be difficult to adjust to these differences? Remember, you would have to do everything in a completely different language too.

## Sleuth Work

**Gather Evidence** How does a day at school in Japan compare to your school day in the United States? Write down evidence from the article to support this.

**Ask Questions** Write three questions you would ask a student from Japan about his or her day at school.

**Make Your Case** Do you think an American student would have more difficulty adapting to a Japanese school or a Japanese student would have more difficulty adapting to an American school? Write a paragraph that supports your opinion.

# Pizza, Pizza Everywhere

Pizza, pizza, pizza!

Everyone loves pizza. Did you know that many Americans eat 23 pounds of pizza a year? Did you know that pepperoni is the most popular pizza topping in the United States?

What kind of pizza is popular in other countries? Get ready to be surprised. It may not be the kind of pizza you're used to ordering!

In Japan, many people love pizza topped with squid, mayonnaise, potatoes, and bacon. In India, people like pizza topped with tandoori chicken, minced mutton (sheep), pickled ginger, or tofu.

In Brazil, green peas are a favorite topping. In Russia, pizza is served with mockba. Mockba is sardines, mackerel, tuna, salmon, and onions. If you want extra fish, you can also add herring.

If you live in France, you might like bacon, onion,

and fresh cream on your pizza. Many people in Pakistan like pizza with curry on it. Fly over to Australia if you want pizza with shrimp, pineapple, and barbecue sauce.

Do you like coconut? If you do, you'd probably like the pizza from Costa Rica. And if you're in the Netherlands, you might like pizza with double cheese, double onions, and double beef.

So if you're willing to try different pizza toppings, grab your suitcase and passport! Maybe you can bring those pizza topping ideas back to the United States.

## Sleuth Work

**Gather Evidence** Write three details about how pizzas look and taste different around the world.

**Ask Questions** Write two questions that you might ask a chef about making the best pizza in town.

**Make Your Case** Would you rather eat pizza in the United States or in another country? Explain your opinion with evidence from the text.

63

# The HARLEM RENAISSANCE on Canvas

Once upon a time, African American artists, writers, and musicians joined other African Americans in a neighborhood called Harlem in New York.

In the 1920s and 1930s, many African Americans moved from the South to northern cities. They left rural jobs as servants or farm workers. Others left their jobs as skilled laborers and teachers in southern cities. They moved to cities in the North to find a better life. Here they found jobs along with other opportunities.

Harlem soon had the largest African American population in the United States. African American art, music, and literature became popular. This period became known as the Harlem Renaissance.

This time in history is most famous for literature and music. However, art was also important. Painters showed African Americans in realistic ways. Paintings showed what life was like for African Americans in urban areas.

Palmer Hayden was one of the first African American artists to paint African Americans. Hayden painted people in both the urban North and the rural South. One of his paintings, *The Janitor Who Paints*, shows a woman and her child having their portrait painted.

Laura Wheeler Waring was a portrait painter. Her best-known portraits were of famous people of the

*The Janitor Who Paints* by Palmer Hayden, Smithsonian American Art Museum, Washington, DC

Harlem Renaissance. The writer James Weldon Johnson and the opera singer Marian Anderson were two of her subjects.

Art from the Harlem Renaissance shows how the African American population changed. It shows the move of many African Americans from rural to urban areas. It shows how African American culture had an impact on Harlem and the rest of the country.

# SLEUTH WORK

**Gather Evidence** What evidence can you find to support the idea that the Harlem Renaissance was important to American culture?

**Ask Questions** Which painter would you like to learn more about? Write three questions to guide your research.

**Make Your Case** Would you like to have lived as an artist, writer, or musician in Harlem during the Harlem Renaissance? List reasons to support your answer.

# Unit 6
## Freedom

Calling all Sleuthhounds! In this unit, you will be looking for clues about freedom. Here are some sleuth tips to help you. Enjoy the ride!

# Sleuth Tips

## Gather Evidence

How do sleuths know if a clue is important?

- Sleuths record clues to keep track. They don't always know which clues will lead to an answer.
- Sleuths look for clues that fit together.

## Ask Questions

How do sleuths think of interesting questions to ask?

- Sleuths often ask for more information about a clue. One clue may lead to many others!
- Sleuths think about questions they still have after they read. Not all questions are answered in the text and pictures.

## Make Your Case

How do sleuths learn from other sleuths?

- Sleuths listen to other sleuths to learn about clues they may have missed.
- Sleuths know that sharing ideas is a great way to learn and to find answers!

## Prove It!

How do sleuths prepare to share what they know?

- Sleuths reread what they wrote, edit, and reread again to make it better.
- Sleuths know they improve with practice. Practice makes sharing easier and more enjoyable!

In 1782, the American Bald Eagle became the symbol of the United States. It was chosen because it's a majestic and strong bird. How did this bird get chosen?

After the Declaration of Independence was signed in 1776, a committee was asked to research a symbol for our new country. This committee included Thomas Jefferson, John Adams, and Benjamin Franklin. They presented an illustration of a woman called "Liberty" holding a shield.

Congress wasn't impressed. It turned to a Philadelphia artist. The artist's design included a Golden Eagle. This species wasn't unique to the United States. After some research, Congress chose the American Bald Eagle. Today, the eagle is pictured on our country's seal, money, and on many stamps.

Not everyone liked this symbol. Benjamin Franklin shared his displeasure in a letter to his daughter in 1784. He said, "For my own part I wish the Bald Eagle had not been chosen the Representative of our Country. He is a Bird of bad moral Character."

Franklin felt the American Bald Eagle stole food from other birds and was a coward.

However, Franklin was happy to see that the illustration of the eagle looked more like a turkey. He felt the turkey was a more appropriate symbol. Franklin believed the turkey was courageous in its own way.

Nevertheless, the American Bald Eagle still represents our country. President John F. Kennedy agreed with the Founding Fathers and once wrote, "The fierce beauty and proud independence of this great bird aptly symbolizes the strength and freedom of America."

## Sleuth Work

**Gather Evidence** Write details that Benjamin Franklin used in his argument against the American Bald Eagle as our country's national symbol.

**Ask Questions** If you were on a committee to decide what mammal should be our country's symbol, what questions would you research to inform your decision? Write at least two questions.

**Make Your Case** Do you think the American Bald Eagle is the best symbol for our country? Write a paragraph that supports your opinion.

# FREEDOM FOR ALL

*"I do order and declare that all persons held as slaves within said designated States, and parts of States, are, and henceforward shall be, free . . ."*

These words are from a famous speech made by President Abraham Lincoln in 1862. The speech is called the Emancipation Proclamation. This speech said that all enslaved people in the Southern states were to be free beginning on January 1, 1863.

The U.S. was in the middle of the Civil War when Lincoln gave this speech. Some states in the South wanted to make their own new country. The states in the North didn't want that to happen. The Northern states and Southern states went to war against each other. This war was the Civil War.

One of the things they were fighting about was slavery. Most people in the Northern states believed slavery was wrong. Many people in the Southern states thought that slavery should be allowed to continue.

After the Northern soldiers won an important battle in the war, Lincoln made this speech. He said that enslaved people in any state fighting against the North should be free. He also said they should be allowed to join the Northern army. Many of them did. Their contributions helped the North win the war.

The Emancipation Proclamation also led to a new law in the United States in 1865. This new law officially ended slavery in all of the states.

## SLEUTH WORK

**Gather Evidence** Abraham Lincoln is an important person in U.S. history. Make a list of facts from this article that helps explain why he is important.

**Ask Questions** Write two questions you might ask Abraham Lincoln about being President during the Civil War.

**Make Your Case** Did President Lincoln have the right to issue the Emancipation Proclamation, knowing that he was going against the laws of several states? State reasons that support your point of view.

# A Performance in a Flash

Have you ever heard of a flash mob? It's a group of people who plan a "surprise" performance in a public place. They agree to meet in a certain location, such as a shopping mall, at a set time. When that time comes, they perform for whoever is around at the time. They often perform a song or dance. Then, when the performance is over, they act as if nothing has happened. Their "audience" includes people who were not in on the secret but just happen to be at the same place at the same time.

Flash mobs are a type of performance art. Many have become Internet hits, with millions of people watching videos of the performances.

Bill Wasik came up with the idea of the flash mob in 2003. He said it was a "social experiment." He wanted to see what would happen. He shared his idea through emails. In June 2003, 200 people showed up at a department store, and they asked the salespeople for help finding something. Then they all left ten minutes later. News of the mob spread through the media.

Wasik's next flash mob took place over two weeks later. Again, the media covered the event. The idea of flash mobs spread across the world within just a couple of months.

Today, flash mobs are so popular you may be able to find the details of one in your area on the Internet. You might decide to join them in the fun!

## Sleuth Work

**Gather Evidence** How did Bill Wasik's idea become such a sensation? Write down evidence from the article.

**Ask Questions** Write three interesting questions you would ask Bill Wasik about flash mobs.

**Make Your Case** Should people be allowed to put on a flash mob performance anywhere they choose? Write a paragraph that includes examples and supports your opinion.

# Lin's Lesson

"You know you're not supposed to bring food downstairs," Mom said to Lin. She was walking up the stairs from Lin's bedroom holding a plate of dried-up sandwich. "When you leave food out, bugs come, and I can't stand bugs. If you want a snack, eat it upstairs."

"Yes, Mom," Lin said, only half paying attention. He didn't see what the big deal was and why she was so worried about bugs. The few he'd seen in his room were harmless little ants. Sometimes when he was drawing, he got so preoccupied that he forgot about the snacks he had brought downstairs.

The next morning, Lin woke up to a strange sensation. He opened his eyes and saw ants crawling over his arm. Lin bolted out of bed. Ants were crawling on the floor and in and out of the pretzel bag that was open on his desk. Lin ran upstairs, where he found his mom drinking her morning cup of tea.

"Mom!" Lin howled. "There are ants all over my room, even in my bed! I never thought this would happen!"

"Oh, Lin," Mom replied, "that's why we have rules—to avoid just this kind of thing. I'll have to call the exterminator, and you'll have to save your allowance and pay me back. Got it?"

"Yes, Mom. I'm really sorry." Lin had learned his lesson the hard way! He would have to use his own money to pay to get the ants removed.

## Sleuth Work

**Gather Evidence** Did Lin learn a lesson? How do you know? Write three details from the text that support your answer.

**Ask Questions** Write three questions you think Lin and his mom would ask each other about this experience a week after it happened.

**Make Your Case** Should parents make children pay for damages that children cause by not following the rules? Write your opinion and give two reasons to support it.

# A Community Spring Break

The snow had melted, and everyone was talking about plans for their spring break trips. Instead, I was sticking around school with some classmates in Mr. Monroe's room. We were excited (really excited) about being a part of Huffman Elementary School's Community Spring Break. Rather than going on vacation, we were giving back to our community. We were helping to make our community a better place to live.

On the first day, we visited a retirement home. Mr. Monroe talked with us about the importance of respecting elders and using good manners when we visited the home. I spoke with a resident named Ms. Rose, and she showed me how to make paper flowers.

The next few days we worked around town. We picked up trash on Front Street. We painted a mural on a wall to discourage people from spray-painting on it. We unpacked boxes of canned goods at the food pantry. Every night I came home tired but feeling good inside.

On Friday afternoon, we went to the courthouse. We thought this was our final project, but when we saw our family, friends, principal, and even Ms. Rose gathered there, we knew something was up.

Our principal stepped up to a podium. "Good afternoon!" she said. "Thank you all for being here today to honor a group of young citizens who have set a wonderful example for our community."

Everyone cheered. A reporter snapped our photo for the newspaper. The headline would read "A Different Kind of Spring Break."

## Sleuth Work

**Gather Evidence** What are some qualities of a good citizen? Make a list using evidence from the story and your own experiences.

**Ask Questions** Write three questions you would need to ask if you were planning a Community Spring Break in your area.

**Make Your Case** Would a vacation or participating in a Community Spring Break be more interesting? Write a paragraph that supports your answer.

# Acknowledgments

## Photographs

Every effort has been made to secure permission and provide appropriate credit for photographic material. The publisher deeply regrets any omission and pledges to correct errors called to its attention in subsequent editions.

Unless otherwise acknowledged, all photographs are the property of Pearson Education, Inc.

Photo locators denoted as follows: Top (T), Center (C), Bottom (B), Left (L), Right (R), Background (Bkgd)

## Cover

Chandler Digital Art

4 (TL) ©kontur-vid/Fotolia, (Bkgrd) ©Nightman1965/Fotolia, (TR) ©PaulPaladin/Fotolia, (CR) ©Warakorn/Fotolia, (BR) ©Zedcor Wholly Owned/Thinkstock, (C) Shutterstock; 5 (TR) Fotolia, (BR) Hemera Technologies/Thinkstock; 8 (B) ©Africa Studio/Fotolia, (CL) ©Marco Birn/Fotolia, (BL) Blindekuh Zurich; 9 (TR) ©Olesia Sarycheva/Fotolia, (CR) PhotoObjects/Thinkstock; 10 (B) ©Constock/Thinkstock, (L) ©Olga Sapegina/Fotolia; 11 (R) ©dinostock/Fotolia, (T) ©Oleksandr Moroz/Fotolia; 12 (Bkgrd) ©Andrew Watson/Fotolia, (T) ©UryadnikovS/Fotolia; 14 (BR) ©Robert Cross/KRT/NewsCom, (C, Bkgrd) Comstock/Thinkstock; 15 (R) ©Carolyn K Smith MD/Fotolia; 16 (TL) ©Aleksandr Vasilyev/Fotolia, (Bkgrd) ©Aptyp-koK/Fotolia, (B) ©Creatas/Thinkstock; 17 (R) ©Andres Rodriguez/Fotolia, (R) ©Philippe Devanne/Fotolia; 20 (T) ©avdwolde/Fotolia, (BL) ©DK Images, (T) ©Eric Isselee/Fotolia, (T) ©estima/Fotolia, (T) ©Felix Mizioznikov/Fotolia, (T) ©Paul Murphy/Fotolia, (T) ©Ulrich Muller/Fotolia, (B) Kuttelvaserova/Shutterstock; 21 (CR) ©Getty Images/Thinkstock, (T) ©ingridd313/Fotolia, (T) ©Lars Christensen/Fotolia, (T) ©Melissa Schalke/Fotolia, (T) ©Oleg Kozlov/Fotolia, (T) ©ptholomeo/Fotolia, (C) ©Rod Planck/Photo Researchers, Inc., (T) ©seraphic06/Fotolia; 22 (BL) ©Everett Collection Inc/Alamy Images, (TR) Steve Petteway/The Collection of the Supreme Court of the United States; 23 (T, B) Prints & Photographs Division, Library of Congress; 24 (B) ©Brad Pict/Fotolia, (T) ©Rob/Fotolia, (T) Carlos Caetano/Shutterstock; 25 (B) ©Michael Flippo/Fotolia, (C) ©Stockbyte/Thinkstock, (R) Fotolia; 26 (BL) ©Stockbyte/Thinkstock, (T) Shutterstock; 27 (R) ©Jupiterimages/Thinkstock, (B) ©Thomas Northcut/Thinkstock; 28 (R) ©Dmitry Petrenko/Fotolia, (Bkgrd) ©freehand/Fotolia, (BL) ©Stefan Ekernas/Fotolia, (Bkgrd) matamu/Fotolia; 29 (TR) ©Bastos/Fotolia, (BR) ©Martin Lodemore/Fotolia; 32 (B) ©Lijuan Guo/Fotolia, (T) ©luciezizkov/Fotolia, (T) ©sarsmis/Fotolia; 33 (BR) ©Fanfo/Fotolia, (R) ©Kirill_M/Fotolia; 34 (BL) ©fotorich/Fotolia, (Bkgrd) ©Igor Podgorny/Fotolia, (C) ©Jennifer Elizabeth/Fotolia; 35 (TR) ©mirvav/Fotolia; 36 (B) ©Ljupco Smokovski/Fotolia, (Bkgrd) Comstock/Thinkstock, (B) Getty Images; 37 (T, C, B) ©DK Images; 38 (T) ©lunamarina/Fotolia, (B) ©Skyline/Fotolia, (Bkgrd) ©Tim Cuff/Alamy Images; 39 (R) ©Tersina Shieh/Fotolia; 40 (T) ©Alfrendo Nature/Thinkstock, (C) ©Hemera Technologies/Thinkstock, (Bkgrd) ©Nat Ulrich/Fotolia, (B) ©Tony Campbell/Fotolia, (BL) ©Vilmos Varga/Fotolia; 41 (R) ©Nikolai Sorokin/Fotolia, (B) ©Paul Hill/Fotolia; 44 (L) ©Glen Jones/Fotolia, (C) ©Vladislav Gajic/Fotolia; 45 (BR) ©Marianne deJong/Fotolia, (TR) Bananastock/Thinkstock; 46 (T) ©davidtui/Fotolia, (T) ©Printing Society/Fotolia, (L) ©Rob/Fotolia, (Bkgrd) ©vlads/Fotolia; 47 (R) ©Kenneth Sponsler/Fotolia; 48 (TL) ©Uros Medved/Fotolia, (C) ©Witold Krasowski/Fotolia, (L) Comstock/Thinkstock, (BL) Hemera Technologies/Thinkstock, (Bkgrd) Juliterimages/Thinkstock; 49 (TR, B) ©Volodymyr Khodaryev/Fotolia, (C) Hemera Technologies/Thinkstock, (BR, B) Thinkstock; 50 (T) ©Everett Collection Inc/Alamy Images; 51 (C) ©MTC Media/Fotolia; 52 (T) ©Anita P. Peppers/Fotolia, (C) ©Natalia Danecker/Fotolia, (Bkgrd) ©SuriyaPhoto/Fotolia, (B) Shutterstock; 53 (R) ©Duncan Noakes/Fotolia, (C) ©Stockbyte/Thinkstock; 56 (C) ©Olga Dmi/Fotolia, (C) Fotolia; 57 (T) ©Radu Razvan/Fotolia, (R) Thinkstock; 58 (T) ©Tinnakorn Nukul/Fotolia, (Bkgrd) ©xiaoloangge/Fotolia; 59 (L) ©canakris/Fotolia, (B) ©Jens Ottoson/Fotolia, (TR) ©uckyo/Fotolia; 60 ©joanna wnuk/Fotolia, (L) ©paylessimages/Fotolia, (T) Shutterstock; 61 (R) ©Etien/Fotolia, (CR) ©japolia/Fotolia, (C) ©paylessimages/Fotolia; 62 (C) ©Alexey Astakhov/Fotolia, (Bkgrd) ©Kitch Bain/Fotolia, (BL) ©Vyacheslav Baranov/Fotolia, (TL, C) Hemera Technologies/Thinkstock, (C) Photodisc/Thinkstock; 63 (BL) ©arkpo/Fotolia, (BR) ©muro/Fotolia, (R) Ryan McVay/Getty Images; 64 (L) ©klavlav/Fotolia, (L) ©zagart117/Fotolia, (Bkgrd) Hemera Technologies/Thinkstock; 65 (BR) ©Rusian Olinchuk/Fotolia, (T) Hemera Technologies/Thinkstock, (T) Smithsonian American Art Museum, Washington, DC, U.S.A./Art Resource, NY; 68 (TL, CL, BL) ©rock76/Fotolia, (R) Comstock/Thinkstock, (B) Prints & Photographs Division, Library of Congress; 69 (BR) ©mattesimages/Fotolia, (BC) ©Sergey Yarochkin/Fotolia, (CR) ©Vladimir Wrangel/Fotolia, (TR) Prints & Photographs Division, Library of Congress; 70 (Bkgrd) ©ilolab/Fotolia, (C) ©Jorg Hackemann/Fotolia; 71 (B) ©steheap/Fotolia; 72 (Bkgrd) ©Chris Jobs/Alamy Images; 74 (L) ©Brand X Pictures/Thinkstock, (TC) ©Judex/Fotolia, (Bkgrd) ©tuja66/Fotolia, (BR) ©Tupungato/Fotolia, (TL) Hemera Technologies/Thinkstock; 75 (C) ©Brad Pict/Fotolia, (BL) ©Jim Barber/Fotolia, (BR) ©LesCunliffe/Fotolia, (CR) Photos/Thinkstock; 76 (BL) ©Toniflap/Fotolia, (BR) Comstock/Thinkstock, (TR) Digital Vision/Thinkstock; 77 (TR) Aramanda/Fotolia.